UNIVERSE to GOD

The Ancient Wisdom of Sages For Children

Anuradha Adarsh

AWS
ANCIENT WISDOM OF THE SAGES

Universe to God

by

Anuradha Adarsh

BLUEROSE PUBLISHERS

India | U.K.

Copyright © Anuradha Adarsh 2023

All rights reserved by author. No part of this publication may be reproduced, stored in a retrieval system or transmitted in any form or by any means, electronic, mechanical, photocopying, recording or otherwise, without the prior permission of the author. Although every precaution has been taken to verify the accuracy of the information contained herein, the publisher assumes no responsibility for any errors or omissions. No liability is assumed for damages that may result from the use of information contained within.

BlueRose Publishers takes no responsibility for any damages, losses, or liabilities that may arise from the use or misuse of the information, products, or services provided in this publication.

For permissions requests or inquiries regarding this publication, please contact:
BLUEROSE PUBLISHERS
www.BlueRoseONE.com
info@bluerosepublishers.com

+91 8882 898 898
+4407342408967
ISBN: 978-93-5819-764-8
Cover design: Muskan Sachdeva
Typesetting: Rohit
First Edition: December 2023

"Our children are the gifts
Given by the mercy of the Lord.
They are delicate,
Take care of them
With love and devotion,
By imparting upon them
The ancient wisdom of sages."

The Indian system of ancient wisdom has disappeared over time. From Vedic knowledge to the power of chanting mantras, the impact of the sound of 'OM' into our lives or the essence of the journey of the soul, the emphasis of ancient wisdom has been lost.

The Ancient Wisdom of the Sages is eternal. Having said that, after the Indian invasion post the 6th century, this ancient education was at the start of destruction. By the time of the 18th century, while the Britishers came into rule, this way of life and education was completely destroyed.

Many gurus of various ashrams constantly work to bring back the lost light of this miraculous education system.

In our advent to bring back this lost fervor, we believe that the right age to introduce the ancient wisdom of the sages into our children is right from the age of 6. Starting from the very basic of concepts, we strive to conduct our classes in such a way that the higher knowledge of absolute truth will be reasized by children as they grow. It should be considered as a course and should be added in the curriculum of schools. A simple dedication of one weekly class will go a long way, helping in character building of children at the right age.

We are here to re-instill the ancient wisdom of the sages, simplified and adaptive to a child's mind.

Universe to God

Dedication

With humility, love, respect, and gratitude, I dedicate this book to my beloved husband, Shri Adarsh Kumar, the inspiration behind my success in life and career. His constant encouragement, guidance, and motivation inspired me to take up AWS to glorious heights.

Anuradha Adarsh

CONTENTS

Preface		viii
Introduction		ix
What to Expect from the course		x
Inspiration Page		xi
कौन है इसको करने वाला		xii

Wisdom Pages   Chapters

1	Wisdom Page 1	About Universe	2
2	Wisdom Page 2	About Om	4
3	Wisdom Page 3	About Om Ma Ni Pad Me Hum	6
4	Wisdom Page 4	About Gayathri Mantra	8
5	Wisdom Page 5	About Flower of Life	10
6	Wisdom Page 6	About Chakra Healing	12
7	Wisdom Page 7	About God Page	14
8	Wisdom Page 8	About Prayer	16
9	Wisdom Page 9	About Mahavakyas	18
10	Wisdom Page 10	About All Wisdom Pages	20
11	Wisdom Page 11	About Prayer	22
12	Wisdom Page 1A	Origin of Universe	24
13	Wisdom Page 2A	Description of OM	27
14	Wisdom Page 3A	Story of Prince to God	30
15	Wisdom Page 4A	Story of King to Brahmarishi	32

CONTENTS

	Wisdom Pages	Chapters	
16	Wisdom Page 5A	More About Flower of Life	34
17	Wisdom Page 6A	More About Chakra Healing	35
18	Wisdom Page 9A	Description of Mahavakyas	36
19	Wisdom Page 9A	Aham Brahmasmi	37
20		Poem	38
21		About Author	39
22		Gallery	40
23		Namaste	44

Preface

It gives me great pleasure to present this book to our esteemed readers.

What is Ancient Education, and what happened to it?

The Gurukul system of Indian education, derived from the ancient scriptures, was scientifically and spiritually conceived to provide a balance between human beings and society. This helped India prosper, and its people were known to be happy and civilized. However, with the passage of time and the arrival of foreign rulers, the wealth of knowledge was exploited for their own gains, resulting in the destruction or loss of invaluable teachings.

Why Ancient Wisdom Of Sages (AWS)?

These life lessons have been passed down through the ages via 'Shruti' or verbal communication by the ancient sages. The practices of meditation, yoga, chanting of the OM sound, and the realization of the existence of God or a supreme power have brought numerous benefits to humanity. Today's children need to understand their roots and acquire wisdom through this simplified, activity-based, and enjoyable form of education. Emphasis is placed on instilling good habits, character formation, and concentration in their pursuits.

In the present era, our children are the youth of tomorrow. It is essential for them to understand their origins and gain wisdom through an education system that is simplified, activity-based, and enjoyable. The development of good habits begins at an early age. We focus on building character, developing personalities, and teaching life lessons. This enables us to nurture individuals of exceptional character, bringing pride to humanity and fostering happiness and peace.

Vision

Our vision is to disseminate the correct knowledge of the ancient wisdom of the sages (our Vedas and Upanishads) worldwide, for the peace and happiness of every human being.

Mission

Spread awareness of ancient scriptures to children through online and offline workshops.

Implement a compulsory curriculum from UKG to PG that focuses on character development in children.

Conduct workshops for parents, highlighting the importance of early exposure to scriptures.

Publish books, workbooks, and online content through web-based platforms to further our cause.

Anuradha Adarsh

Introduction

Ancient Wisdom of Sages (AWS) for children is a course designed to be easily grasped by children aged 6 to 14, starting from the very basics, enabling them to realize the eternal truth.

Course 1 is an endeavor to guide children on their journey from the Universe to God. Throughout this course, children learn about:

1. The Universe
2. The creator of the Universe
3. Understanding God
4. The abode of God
5. The power of the sound "OM"
6. The significance of Mantras
7. Exploring Chakras and Healing

In AWS, we believe that education is not just about acquiring knowledge but also about character development, self-control, confidence, and understanding social issues. Our approach to education emphasizes holistic development encompassing physical, mental, and spiritual aspects, aiming for purity of character.

Course 1 comprises wisdom pages from Page 1 to Page 9, along with engaging stories related to these wisdom pages.

This book simplifies the essence of Ancient Scriptures, and we strongly believe that everyone should have the opportunity to learn from it.

Our goal is to integrate our courses as a subject in the school curriculum. We propose introducing one class per week dedicated to character building for children at the right age.

What to expect from the course?

Every parent envisions a child who:

1. Respects their parents and all elders.
2. Possesses a clear understanding of their life goals and how to achieve them.
3. Has a comprehensive understanding of basic human values.
4. Respects all religions, holds a deep love for God, and believes in the essence of humanity.
5. Demonstrates confidence, competence, and intelligence.

Society will benefit from individuals who:

1. Embrace the welfare and importance of harmony.
2. Respect one another and actively work towards the betterment of society.

The nation will benefit from individuals who:

1. Take pride in their country and strive to establish and enhance its global stature.
2. Display selfless determination to develop the nation.
3. Possess environmental awareness.
4. Serve as ideal assets for the future of our country.

Ancient wisdom of the sages

Inspired by Kritik

We are learning the ancient wisdom of the sages for children – it gives us correct knowledge of human nature.

Myself Kritik, along with my 5 year old sister Kimmaya and granny Anuradha have prepared the program to help build character in children.

My dream is to see the program being taught compulsorily in our schools as a course subject.

This Program has four parts

- ❖ True self …..we learn ….good and bad habits.
- ❖ Self exploration…..we know our self
- ❖ Self realisation ….we realise our self
- ❖ Self transformation-we transform our self

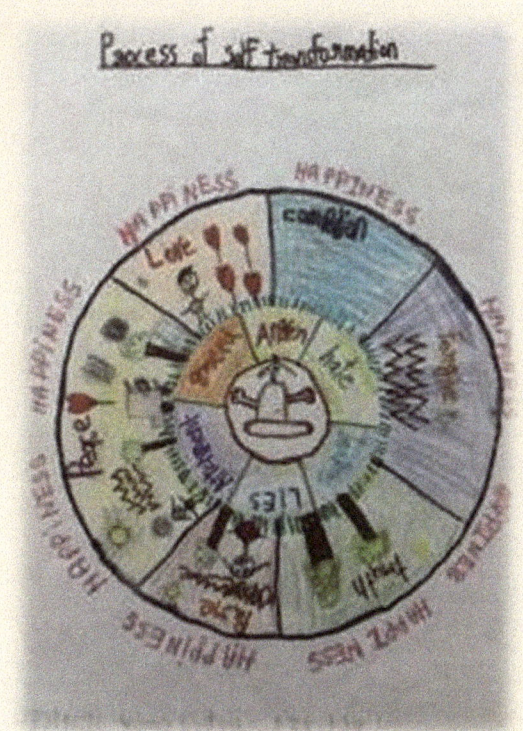

This course removes bad habits, like anger, sad, laziness, lies and greed. Anger destroys everything in life.
This course gives us mastery and concentration
This course teaches us good habits like Truth, happiness to help, love and peace .

This makes us good Human being.

Everybody can not read vedas and this course extract from this ancient wisdom …

This course will transform

The Children of the whole world.

Written by – Kritik
(When he was in 2nd standard, he wrote this Article for his school magazine)

कौन है इसको करने वाला

ये है एक कहानी
जो सब बच्चों को सुनानी
जो नानी को सुनानी जो है नाना को सुनानी

जो दादी को सुनानी जो हैं दादा को सुनानी
ये है एक कहानी जो सब बच्चों को सुनानी...1

चलो चले आकाश को देखे
देखे उसकी नीली चादर
उसमे देखे सुंदर बादल
कभी कभी वो गरज जाते हैं
कभी कभी वो बरस जाते हैं

कौन इसे है करने वाला
कौन है इसको करने वाला...2

देखो सुंदर सूरज आता
सब ओर वो रोशनी लाता
सारे जग को जगमग जगमग करता जाता
सारे आकाश का एक ही सूरज
सारी दुनिया को चमकाता

कौन इसे है करने वाला
कौन है इसको करने वाला....3

अब देखो इस धरती को
घूम घूम कर रात को लाती
चंदा और तारों को हम सब से मिलवाती
रोज़ सवेरा रोज़ अँधेरा
रोज़ सवेरा रोज़ अँधेरा
रोज़ रोज़ हमको दिखालाती

कौन इसे है करने वाला
कौन है इसको करने वाला....4

अब आ जाओ इस धरती पर
सुंदर सागर सुंदर नदियां
सुंदर चिड़िया सुंदर मछली
सुन्दर सुन्दर पशु हैं पक्षी

कौन इसे है करने वाला
कौन है इसको करने वाला...5

सुंदर पौधे सुंदर फूल
ठंडी ठंडी हवा जो बहती
सुंदर सुंदर खुशबू उड़ती

कौन इसे है करने वाला
कौन है इसको करने वाला....6

पूरी दुनिया सुंदर सजायी
पूरे ज्ञान के साथ बनाई
पूरे ज्ञान को पहले लाये
पूरा विज्ञान को पहले लाये
तब तो हम धरती पर आये
तब तो हम धरती पर आये

कौन इसे है करने वाला
कौन है इसको करने वाला....7

आओ चलो पढ़लो ये पुस्तक
आओ चलो समझो यह पुस्तक

कौन इसे है करने वाला
कौन है इसको करने वाला...8

Poem by Mrs.Anuradha Adarsh

Wisdom Page 1 :
TEACHES ABOUT UNIVERSE

Our Story Starts With Universe.

Our story starts with Universe.

It is very curious... from where we come to where we are, it is called the universe.

Do we think all children know a little bit about the universe?

What is the universe?

The universe is everything. It includes all space, matter, energy, and time itself. It includes galaxies with stars, the sun, the moon, the planet on which we live, the air, water, fire, humans, animals, plants, trees, flowers, and everything.

But who made this?

Everything was created by a single supreme divine power or universal energy...

How and when, you will read the story, which indicates the origin of the universe has already been explained by science and ancient scriptures thousands of years ago.

This page is for parents/ grandparents / teachers Please read this page to children

About Universe
Ancient Wisdom of the Sages
for Children
It gives us correct knowledge

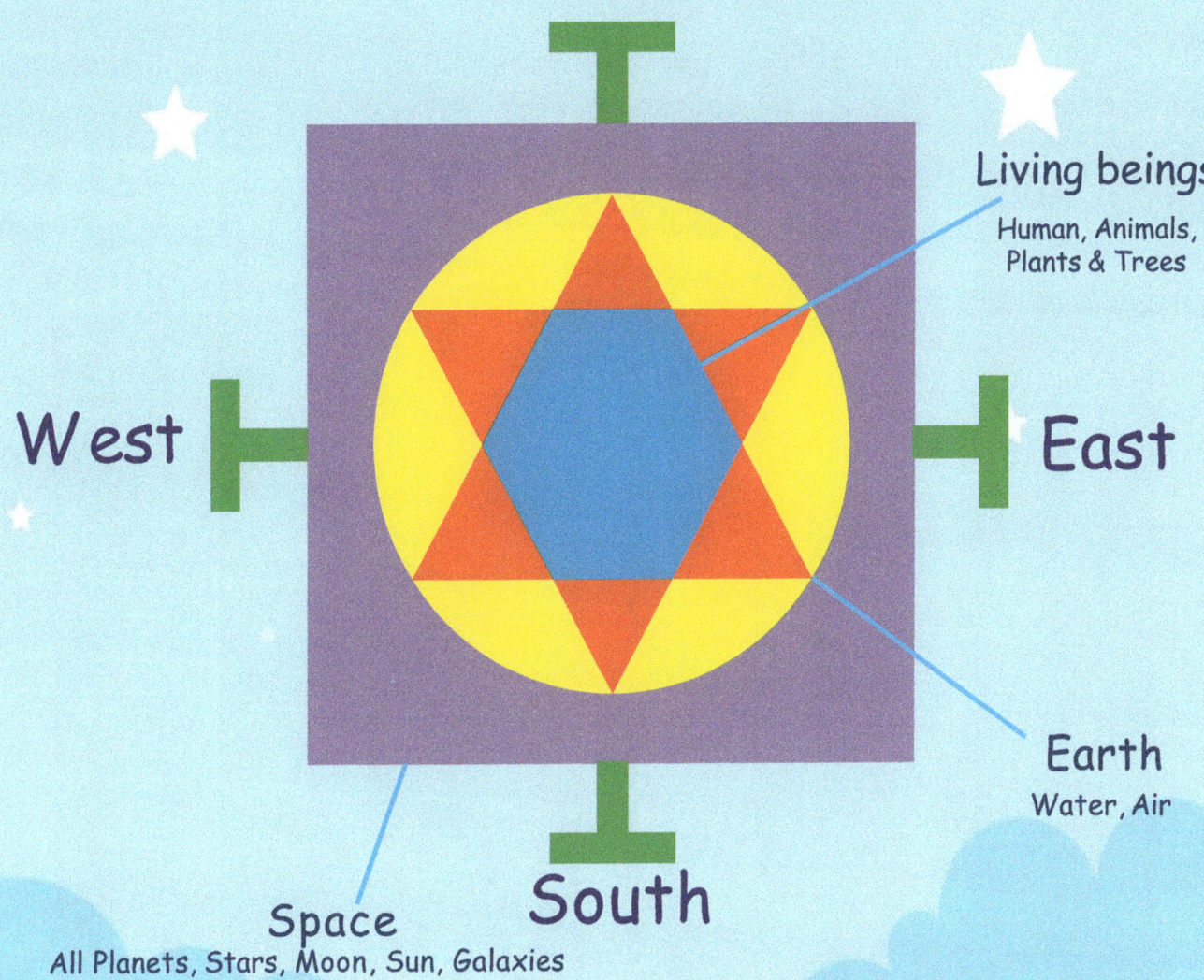

Symbol of Ancient Wisdom

From - Rig veda

Pl Note: This work will be done by children in workbook

Wisdom Page 2
TEACHES ABOUT OM

OM - ॐ

Om is the seed of the whole creation.

Om is one of the most important spiritual sounds. Om is the most sacred symbol and mantra.

Om is the tool of meditation.

Om means many things, it means to love, eternity, purity, and peace. Chanting Om, writing Om, and listening to Om give us concentration. After the concentration, it helps us to receive mastery.

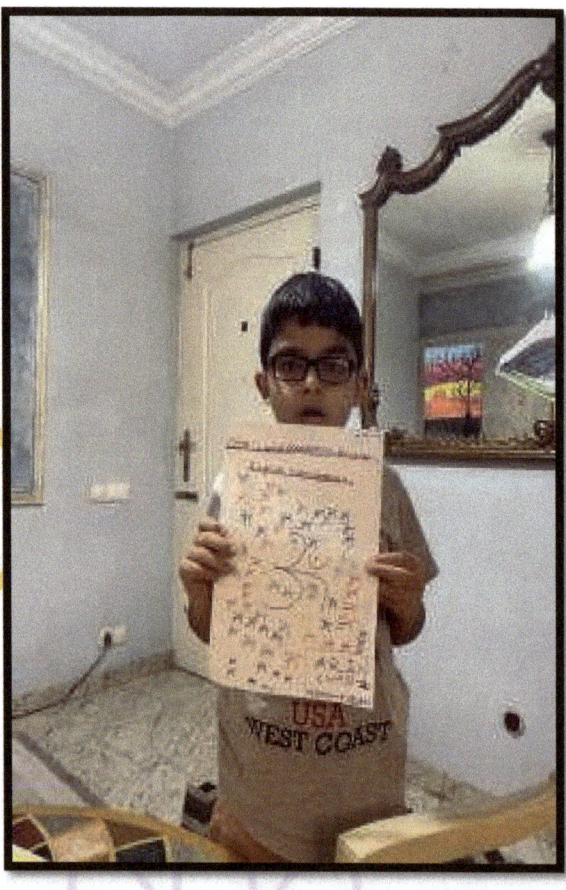 

This page is for parents/ grandparents / teachers Please read this page to children

About Om

Om is the Sound of the Universe
It Gives Concentration

Writing

Chanting

Listening

Patanjali Yoga Sutra

Pl Note: This work will be done by children in workbook

Wisdom Page 3

TEACHES ABOUT OM MA NI PAD ME HUM

Short Story

Buddha, born with the name Siddhartha Gautama, was a teacher, philosopher and spiritual leader who is considered the founder of Buddhism.
Once upon a time. Lord Gautama Buddha was sitting with his disciples and preaching to them. He then told his disciples, Anger is the greatest enemy of everyone. The person who is angry not only hurts himself but also harms others.
He burns in the fire of revenge and ruins his life. He has taught four noble truth and eightfold path.

This page is for parents/ grandparents / teachers Please read this page to children

About Affirmation
Om Ma Ni Pad Me Hum

I am	Om	Generosity
I am	Ma	Ethics
I am	Ni	Patience
I am	Pad	Perseverance
I am	Me	Concentration
I am	Hum	Wisdom

By Lord Buddha

Born in 535 BCE

Got enlightment in 7 Years

Pl Note: This table will be drawn by children in workbook

Wisdom Page 4
TEACHES ABOUT MANTRA

- A mantra is a poetic revelation received by human sages during a state of deep concentration. The essential power of the mantra is to make us see the world as it is to be seen in reality and to be able to think beyond our senses.

- If you remember your mantra, you are free from many things, like being jealous, hateful, angry, and negative. Nothing adverse will ever affect you.

- But remember the mantra when you are silent. Remember your mantra with love. A mantra is like an atomic power and if you rely upon it honestly, it will sooner or later, lead you to the highest peak.

- Your mantra is your real friend in the world.

O divine mother,
may your pure
divine light
illuminate all realms
(physical, mental &
spiritual)
of our being.
Please expel any
darkness from
our hearts and bestow
upon us the
true knowledge.

This page is for parents/ grandparents / teachers Please read this page to children

About Mantra

Gayatri Mantra

Om bhur bhuvaha svaha

Tat savitur varenyam

Bhargo devasya dhimahi

Dhiyo yo nah prachodayat

ॐ भूर् भुवः स्वः।

तत् सवितुर्वरेण्यं।

भर्गो देवस्य धीमहि।

धियो यो नः प्रचोदयात् ॥

Written by
Vishva Mitra
Rigveda 3.62.10 {11}

Pl Note: This work will be done by children in workbook

Wisdom Page 5

TEACHES ABOUT FLOWER OF LIFE

1. The flower of life is believed to be a blueprint of life,
2. Containing the fundamental pattern for everything in the universe
3. From the smallest atoms to the largest galaxies.
4. It is also a representation that everything is connected

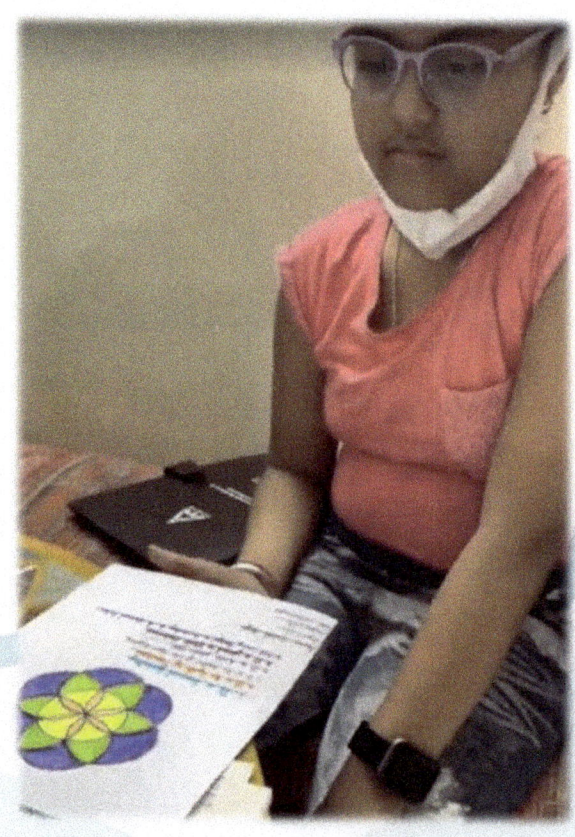

This page is for parents/ grandparents / teachers Please read this page to children

Flower Of Life

- It is Sacred Geometry
- It is The Cycle of Creation
- It is The Symbol of a Major Religions
- It Is 6000 Years Old
- It is found in the Whole Universe
- All Living things is according to its Sacred Ratio

Pl Note: This work will be done by children in workbook

Wisdom Page 6
TEACHES ABOUT CHAKRA

1. Chakras are the wheel or energy circles, In medical science these are endocrine glands and major nerve plexus and arterial plexus.

2. In ancient age, when medical science was not invented, Yogis, Saints, Rishis and Munis invented these chakras.

3. Each chakra indicates the different systems of body.

This page is for parents/ grandparents / teachers Please read this page to children

7 Chakras

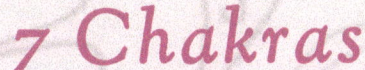

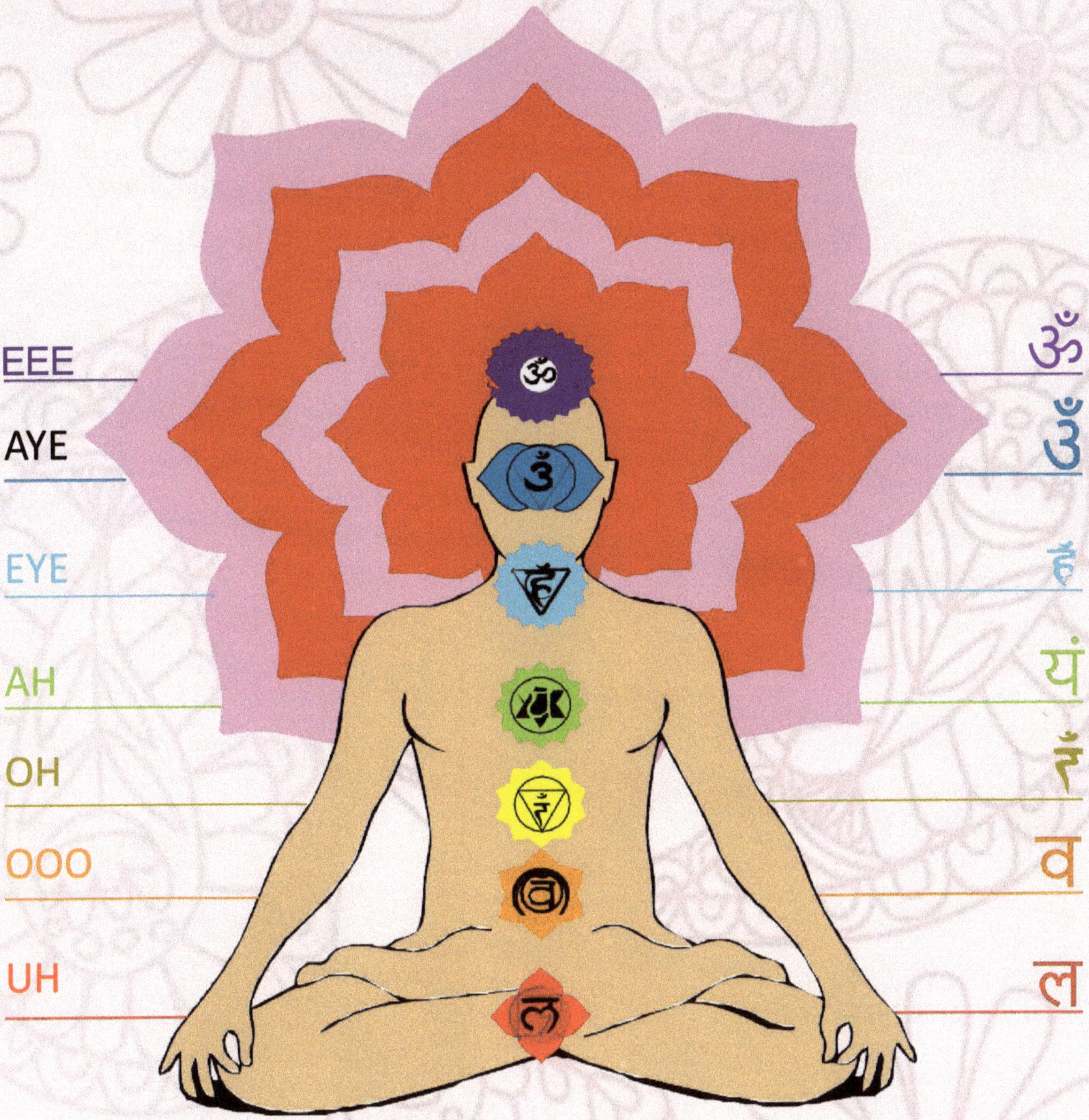

EEE	ॐ
AYE	ॐ
EYE	ह
AH	यं
OH	रं
OOO	व
UH	ल

7 Minute Chakra Healing by Mantra Sound

Rigveda

Pl Note: This work will be done by children in workbook

Wisdom Page 7
TEACHES ABOUT GOD

Who's the one doing it?
Let the story begin now

It's a supreme divine glory,
It's a supreme divine power.
It's a supreme divine knowledge,
It's a supreme divine science.

It's not visible,
But it's found everywhere.
Neither it has the beginning
Nor it has the end.

It is Parabrahma,
   It is Parabrahma

It has thousands of names, It has thousands of forms.

कौन इसे है करने वाला ?
चलो कहानी अब शुरू होती है ।

ये एक दिव्य विभूति है,
ये एक दिव्य शक्ति है।
ये एक दिव्य ज्ञान है,
ये एक दिव्य विज्ञानं है।

ये ना थो दिखाई देता है,
पर हर जगह पर होता है।
ना तो इसका आदि है,
ना तो इसका अंत है।

ये तो परब्रह्म है,
   ये तो परब्रह्म है ।

इसके हजारों नाम है, इसके हजारों रूप है।

This page is for parents/ grandparents / teachers Please read this page to children

About God
Supreme Divine Knowledge
Supreme Divine Power Known As "Brahman or God"

God has many names Brahma, Vishnu, Shiva, Rama, Krishna and More

Brahaman Created the Universe, the Sound OM, the Solar System, the Objects in Space & all living things

Brahman created 4 Scriptures for Human Beings, which gives us Correct Knowledge of the whole World, Character Building & Personality Development.

Rig Veda and Vishnu Puran

Pl Note: This work will be done by children in workbook

Wisdom Page 8
TEACHES ABOUT PRAYER

I AM A SHRINE OF LORD…..
 GOD IS IN ME
I am peace, pure and truth

I AM A SHRINE OF LORD
GOD IS IN ME
I am peace, pure and truth

I AM A SHRINE OF LORD
GOD IS IN ME
I am peace, pure and truth

This page is for parents/ grandparents / teachers Please read this page to children

About Prayer

I AM a Shrine of Lord

Krishna
Durga

God is in Me

Oh God, Give Me Strength

I Will Do all my work with Pure, Peace and Truth

Pure

Peace

Truth

Isha- Upanishad

Pl Note: This work will be done by children in workbook

Wisdom Page 9
TEACHES ABOUT MAHAVAKYAS

Vedas

Rig Veda
Sam Veda
Yajur Veda
Athar Veda

This page is for parents/ grandparents / teachers Please read this page to children

Mahavakyas

- Brahman is Real
  World is Unreal
- Brahman is Supreme
  Divine Knowledge
- Brahman is one without a second
- Brahman and Atman is one
- We are Brahman

अहम् ब्रह्मास्मि

अहम् ब्रह्मास्मि

अहम् ब्रह्मास्मि

Yajur Veda

Pl Note: This work will be done by children in workbook

Wisdom page 10

TEACHES ABOUT ALL WISDOM PAGES

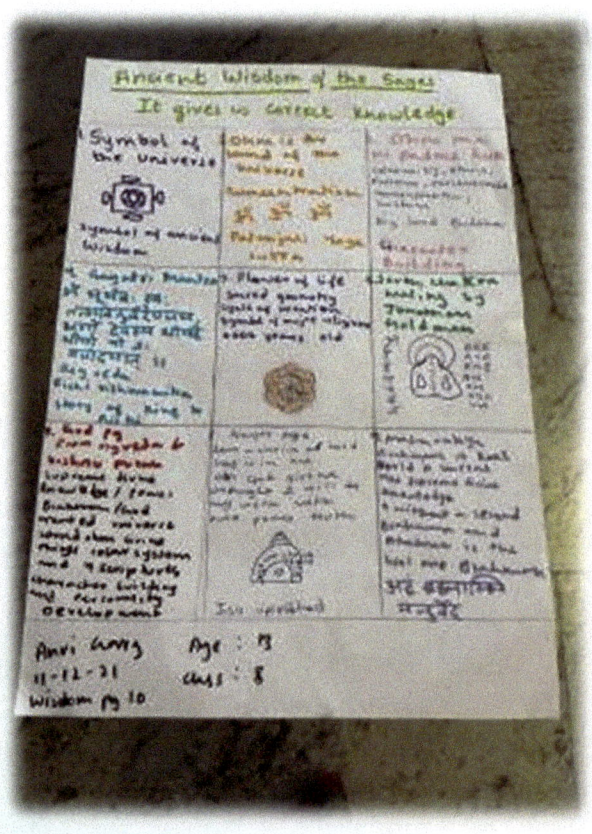

This page is for parents/ grandparents / teachers Please read this page to children

About All Wisdom Pages

Wisdom Page -1 About the Universe	**Wisdom Page -2** Om is the First Sound Of the Universe	**Wisdom Page-3** Om Ma Ni Pad Me Hum Affirmation
Wisdom Page-4 Gayatri Mantra Origin & Meaning	**Wisdom Page-5** Flower of Life Sacred Geometry	**Wisdom Page -6** 7 Chakras Chakra Healing
Wisdom Page-7 God Page Supreme Divine Power & Knowledge	**Wisdom Page -8** Prayer Page I am a Shrine Of Lord God is in me	**Wisdom Page -9** Mahavakyas अहम् ब्रह्मास्मि

Pl Note: This work will be done by children in workbook

Our Prayer
I am a shrine of Lord - God is in me

I Am		**I Am**
PEACE		**PEACE**
PURE		**PURE**
TRUE		**TRUE**

My self
I am a shrine of Lord - God is in me
I am peace pure and truth
Aham Brahmasmi
Aham Brahmasmi
Aham Brahmasmi

Thanks to God
Thank you, God. You made a beautiful universe for us.
Thank you, God. For creating the earth for us to live on.
Thank you, God. You made scriptures, which gives knowledge of the whole universe

Prayer to God
Oh God give me the strength. I do all my work with
Peace, pure and truth.
Oh God, I receive correct knowledge from all directions.
Oh God, I receive noble thoughts from all directions.
Oh God, guide me to the right goal for my life.
Oh God I live happily with my family...

Pl Note: This work will be done by children in workbook
Ancient Wisdom of the sages : Do the prayer 2 times, in the morning and night

UNIVERSE
TO
GOD

Long Story of few of our Wisdom Pages begins.........

About the Universe

We are talking about the origin of the universe….according to Modern Science & Ancient Scriptures. The story covers three steps….

1. Explosion
2. Before Explosion
3. After Explosion

1. Explosion
SCIENCE was discovered in 1925
According to modern science – NASA discovered
There was a VERY big EXPLOSION that happened 13.8 billion years ago, which is known as BIG BANG…..A tiny dense fireball with infinite density exploded due to its internal pressure and heat…. But what caused this explosion, what was before that …..

ANCIENT SCRIPTURE …THOUSANDS OF YEARS AGO …OR TIMELESS …..
The vedic text also suggests that there was a cosmic egg known as Hiranya Garba that exploded. It was known as Brahmand Blast its debris , the universe formed and Rig Veda says , it was infinite universal energy known as "BRAHMAN".

2. BEFORE THE EXPLOSION…. What was there ?
ACCORDING TO ANCIENT SCRIPTURE ….NASADIYA SUKTA, 10TH MANDAL, 12th SUKTA 7 MANTRAS. Nasadiya sukta tells about , what was there before universe was formed…….

Mantra 1
There was nothing existing , no time before creation, nor anything , no sky, no atmosphere what Covered this and who is responsible for this, nos cosmic water.

This page is for parents/ grandparents / teachers Please read this page to children

Mantra 2
There was neither death nor immortality before the creation, no night, no day, no biological life, no Light. no darkness, no sun, no moon, stars or any other planets, nor air.

Mantra 3
Absence of light and space, there was only darkness wrapped in darkness

Mantra 4
In the beginning that descended on it that was Piramal seed born of mind, sages researched their hearts with wisdom

Mantra 5
Then from the seed of desire waves of energy came out like sun rays all around, which started the creation of the universe by joining that eternal substance (Prakriti)

Mantra 6
At present who can tell completely & exactly when and how this variety of creation originated and created because learned people themselves came after creation. Therefore in the present time one cannot describe precisely what was before the creation and what was the reason for its creation.

Mantra 7
What is the source of creation ? Who is its doer ?
The operator of the universe observing is sitting somewhere above in heaven . Know him, O scholars, if you cannot know , then who can ?

3. After the EXPLOSION
Our Universe began with an explosion of space itself- the BIG BANG . Starting from an extremely high density and temperature , space expanded, the universe cooled, and the simplest elements formed. Gravity gradually drew either together to form the first stars, the first galaxies, planets, our earth and so on.

This page is for parents/ grandparents / teachers Please read this page to children

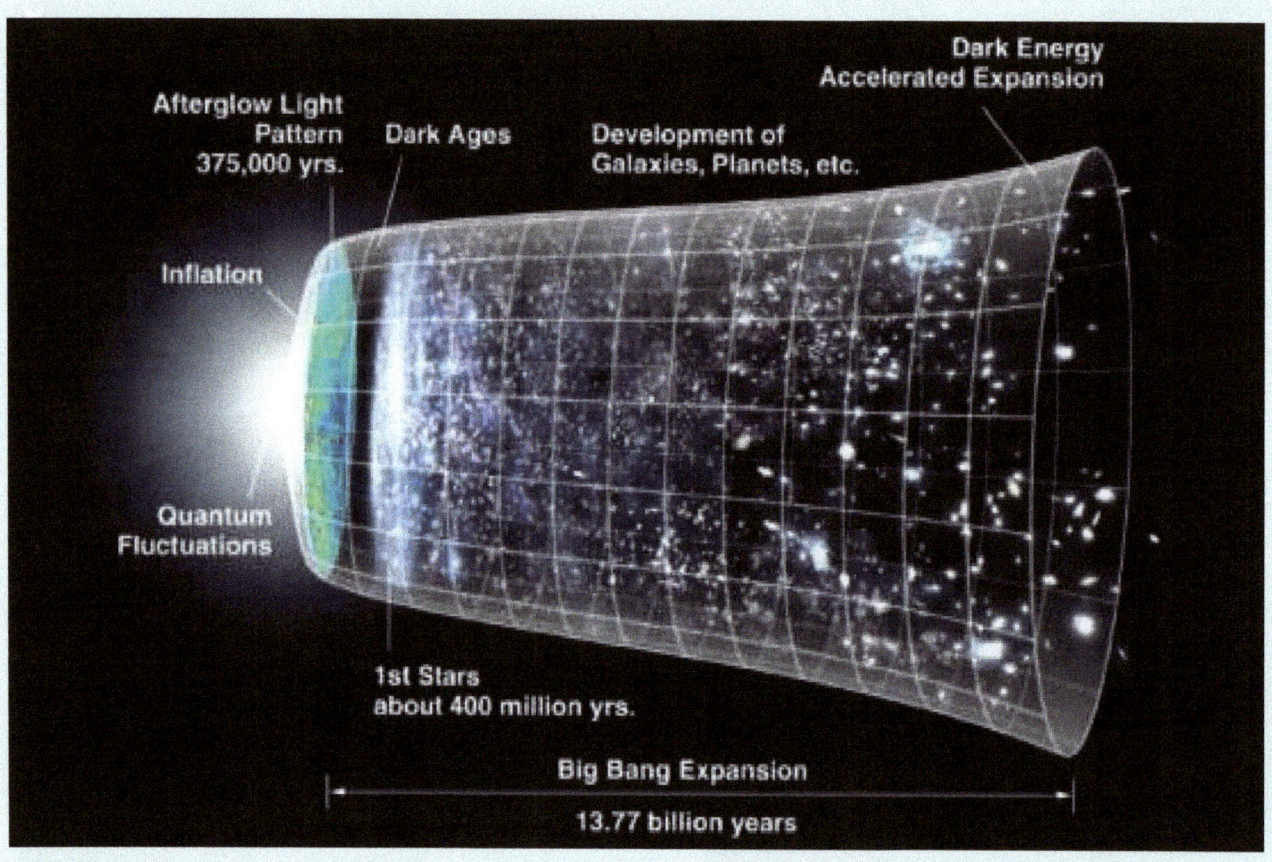

Story to be continued in Series 4.......

This page is for parents/ grandparents / teachers Please read this page to children

Om

About essence of Om from different scriptures

OM IS GOD
Om represents -- Brahman -ataman
OM IS THE SYMBOL OF THE WHOLE WORLD...A-U-M—SILENCE ....
Manduka Upanishad
Om is the bow, the arrow is the Aman, Brahman is the mark, and the arrow becomes one with the mark Brahman....Mundaka Upanishad
Om as all states of time ....Mandukya
Om as all states of atman
Om as all states of consciousness

Om as all of knowledge
Om is a tool of meditation empowering one to know the GOD within one self ...
Om is the most sacred syllable and mantra of brahaman ....Rig Veda
Om is predominant sound of universe ......Rig Veda
Om gives melodic momentum and energy to mantra.......Aitareya brahmana.
Om is beginning of mantra ...
Om is the seed of whole creation ....
Om is exactly the sound same as frequency of earth's rotation on its axis.

This page is for parents/ grandparents / teachers Please read this page to children

Om is eternal Song
Om is the song which is there in universe all the time – – –
Om heard - all the sages in the past when they went deep into meditation
Om means love, eternity, purity, and peace
Om is the seed of whole creation –
Om is the sound of creation in Bible
Om means truth
Om is the name of infinity or divinity
Om is the origin of universe -
Om also called rainbow
Om has several benefit psychological and spiritual

Om chanting symbolise a journey of darkness to Pure light – –
Om found between 1500 to 1200 BC – –
Om chanting will attend your goal, if nothing else works just chant om – –
Om is Primal Song of the universe
Om syllable carrying immense life force energy
Om is a mystic sellable considered the most sacred mantra in Hindi
Om is a seed Mantra
Om is the word of God – – s
Om is the prime mantra – A—invokes Brahma the creative aspect– U—invokes Vishnu the preserver—
M —sound represents the destructive aspect of god shiva .

Om is a powerful tool to focus and quiet the mind
Om is one of the most important spiritual symbols …
OM — Rama is identified with om. Rama is mystic symbol om .you are higher the highest …
Om is shiva
Om connotes the female Divine energy…..
Om is a primal energy, primordial power …
Om is the essence of the Gayatri mantra
Om is the pituitary gland and Penial gland chakra
You are OM …

This page is for parents/ grandparents / teachers Please read this page to children

A	U	M
KRISHNA	VISHNU	RADHA RANI SELF
PAST	PRESENT	FUTURE
CREATION	PRESERVATION	TRANSFORMATION
IMMORALITY	OMNISCIENCE	JOY
CREATIVE ENERGY	PRESERVATIVE ENERGY	DESTRUCTIVE ENERGY
BRAHMA	VISHNU	SHIVA
YAGNA	DANA	TAPAS
RIG VEDA	SAMA VEDA	YAJUR VEDA
EARTH	SPACE	HEAVEN
OBTAINING	EXALTATION	ERECTING
WAKEFUL	DREAM.	DEEP SLEEP
AGNI	VAYU.	ADITYA
BHUR	BHUVAH	SVAH
FOOD	WATER	MOON
INTELLECT	MIND	PSYCHE
BREATH.	FIRE.	SUN
FEMININE.	MASCULINE	NEUTER

This page is for parents/ grandparents / teachers Please read this page to children

Prince To God

A Story of Kindness

Once upon a time, there was a kingdom named Kapilavasthu, ruled by a king named Suddhodana. The king was blessed with a beautiful baby boy named Siddhartha.

After the birth of a baby boy, King Rajpurohit said this boy has a very bright future. He will become a very famous king. He will give birth to a new religion, or Dharma, and spread this dharma in the whole world, and the world will call him God.

Siddhartha was a bright, happy, kind, and gentle child.

The prince grew up and married a beautiful princess, Yashodhara. But Siddhartha was unhappy at the palace.

This page is for parents/ grandparents / teachers Please read this page to children

One day, he told his servant Channa, "Let's go for a ride outside the palace." The prince saw a man bent with age.
A sick man who was crying in agony and a dead body was being carried by a group of people.
The king then asked Channa, "What is this?"
Channa answered that every person who was born, grew up, and eventually died one day
The king was very upset. He left everything and went to the forest in search of answers.
Why do people get sick and die?
The King then visited Alara Kalama, a Guru, and many other Gurus in his quest to find the answers.
But he is not able to get the answer. What is happiness?
Then Siddhartha sat under a tree until he got the answer himself. And he spread the preaching to his disciples, and then people called him Gautam Buddha. Then Gautam Buddha's teachings became dharma known as Buddha dharma.
And Buddha Dharam spread to many countries.
His teachings were very simple; people could learn them easily. After a while, everyone called him God.
That's why a kind prince became a god.

His four noble truths are:
1. Life is full of suffering.
2. Suffering is caused by desire.
3. Humans can free themselves from all that.
4. Truth be told, the way to achieve this freedom

And eightfold path;
The steps of the Noble Eightfold Path are
1. Right understanding,
2. Right Thought
3. Right speech
4. Right Action
5. Right Livelihood
6. Right Effort
7. Right mindfulness
8. Right Concentration

This page is for parents/ grandparents / teachers Please read this page to children

King to Brahmarishi

Story of - Greed, Anger, Ego, jealous & Comparison

Thousands of years ago there was once a kind and generous king named Kaushik who was touring his kingdom. Near the end of his tour he came across an ashram lead by Vashisht Rishi. He and his army were invited to have a meal at the ashram, the rishi called a cow named Nandini who made many delicious dishes for them

Greed:
Here he had greed , the king wanted the cow for himself so he asked politely but he was refused.

Anger:
Here he had Anger, so he used force but he was unable to take Nandini since she was god's cow.

He thought '*Is spiritual power stronger than Physical power?*' He went and prayed to Shiva and received power stronger than physical powers of air, water, and fire and tried to defeat the rishi.

EGO:
Here he had EGO, after a long fight he lost, so he went and prayed to Brahma.

Jealousy:
Here he had Jealousy, he wished to be a rishi which was granted. He still couldn't defeat the rishi.

Comparison:
Here he had Comparison, so he prayed to Vishnu and asked to be a Brahmarishi.

Now he lost all his greed, anger ego, jealousy and comparison and didn't want Nandini anymore. He became a Brahmarishi, God gave him revelation which came out of his mouth as Gayatri Mantra. Since then he is known as Vishwamitra.

Gayatri Mantra

Om bhur bhuvaha svaha
Tat savitur varenyam
Bhargo devasya dhimahi
Dhiyo yo nah prachodayat

ॐ भूर् भुवः स्वः।
तत् सवितुर्वरेण्यं।
भर्गो देवस्य धीमहि।
धियो यो नः प्रचोदयात् ॥

This page is for parents/ grandparents / teachers Please read this page to children

Flower of Life

The flower of life represents the universe, and each of the circles represents a part of the world. It is a circle, which itself contains several of the same sizes and is connected by their center. When we look at this figure, we get the impression that we see flowers, whereas, in reality, they are circles.

Many cultures and civilizations around the world consider the flower of life motif to be very powerful.

The symbol of the Flower of Life has been found on many ancient relics, rock faces, and monuments throughout the world from East to West.
It is widely used in religious and meditation places.

The flower of life was discovered on Assyrian relics dating back to 645 BC. The symbol also appears on the walls of the temple of Osiris in Abydos and is engraved in red ochre by the civilization of ancient Egypt.

The flower of life has several advantages. It is best known for its spiritual fields.

The flower of life spreads energy that contributes to the harmonization of the environment. It also has the virtues of regeneration, balance, dynamism, and protection.

This page is for parents/ grandparents / teachers Please read this page to children

Chakra

1. Chakras are the wheel or energy circles.
2. In medical science these are endocrine glands and major nerve plexus and arterial plexus

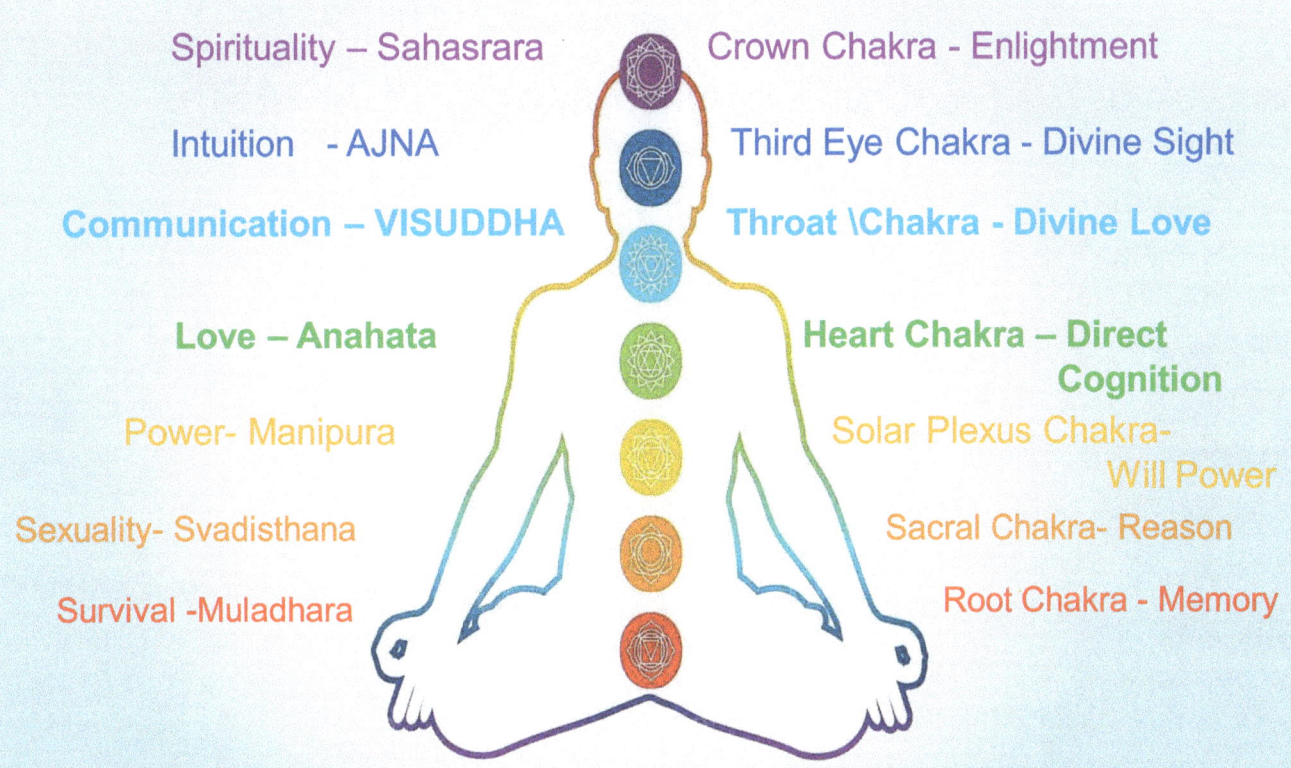

Spirituality – Sahasrara   Crown Chakra - Enlightment
Intuition – AJNA   Third Eye Chakra - Divine Sight
Communication – VISUDDHA   Throat Chakra - Divine Love
Love – Anahata   Heart Chakra – Direct Cognition
Power – Manipura   Solar Plexus Chakra - Will Power
Sexuality – Svadisthana   Sacral Chakra - Reason
Survival – Muladhara   Root Chakra - Memory

Mantra Sound – English	Mantra Sound - Sanskrit	Colour	God	Location
EEE	ॐ	Purple	Shiva	Top of the head
AYE	ॐ	Dark Blue	Bramhani	Centre of the forehead
EYE	ह	Light Blue	Panchavaktra Shiva	Throat
AH	यं	Green	Vayu	Heart
OH	रं	Yellow	Vishnu	Stomach
OOO	व	Orange	Vishnu	Belly Button
UH	ल	Red	Indra	Root of spine

This page is for parents/ grandparents / teachers Please read this page to children

Mahavakyas

- Mahavakyas are great contemplation and great sentences.

- Contemplation means – thoughtful observation, full of deep consideration, hard thinking about **GOD**

- These make wisdom more accessible

- Validation in the inner laboratory

- Start by hearing, the inner inside that is described as direct experience, not mere your belief.

- Over and over and over compassion practices

- Mahavakyas are the heart of Vedanta

- Contemplation makes one aware of existence of the reality

  अहम् ब्रह्मास्मि

This page is for parents/ grandparents / teachers Please read this page to children

Aham Brahmasmi

Atman

Supreme Divine Knowledge
Supreme Divine Immortal Power
who made and control the
Universe including Us is
Brahman

We

AUM is the bow; Atman is the arrow.
Brahman is the target;
Aim precisely such that the arrow
Become merged with the target.

Anuradha Adarsh

Yajurveda
Mundaka Upanishad
Canto 2 - Verse 4

एन्सिएंट विजडम

संसार में दुःख का कारण क्या ?
संताप शोक का निवारण क्या?

इस खोज में बच्चे निकल पड़े
एन्सिएंट विजडम वो पढने लगे!

अच्छे और सच्चे बनने लगे
उन्हें देख बड़े भी बदलने लगे!

भय और आलस खत्म हुआ
लालच और ईर्ष्या घटने लगी
क्रोध घृणा भी हटने लगी!

सब कर्म करे सब कर्म करे
दुनिया में खुशियां बढ़ने लगी

दुनिया अच्छी अब होने लगी
दुनिया सच्ची अब होने लगी!

अब प्रेम ही प्रेम बिखरने लगा
सब साथ साथ में रहने लगे

पूरी दुनिया में सुख ही सुख
सुख ही सुख और सुख ही सुख!

Poem by Kimaya

(She wrote this poem during Corona, at the age of 5)

About The Author

Mrs. Anuradha Adarsh, the author of this book, has a noble mission with the creation of Ancient Wisdom of Sages (AWS): to reintroduce ancient scriptures to today's generation, believing that they hold the key to guiding children, youth, and adults towards the ultimate truth.

Born on July 19, 1955, in Meerut, she displayed remarkable business acumen from a young age and achieved great success as an entrepreneur, earning numerous prestigious awards. Despite reaching great heights and enjoying a luxurious life, she found her purpose when her grandchildren, Kritik and Kimmaya, questioned her about the nature of existence and the possibility of shaping a brighter, happier, and more peaceful future.

Inspired by their inquiries, she realized the importance of introducing the wisdom of ancient scriptures to the younger generation, providing them with clarity and answers to their doubts. For eight years, she immersed herself in the study of these scriptures and eventually launched the Ancient Wisdom of Sages for Children, presenting the profound teachings in easily understandable English.

Her endeavor is to give back to society by disseminating these teachings through this platform. The core motto of AWS is to eliminate ignorance, ego, jealousy, and selfishness from the lives of children, youth, and adults, guiding them towards the ultimate destination of absolute truth, and she aims to integrate these teachings into today's education system.

Work done by the Author

 **Calendar:** The calendar for the year comes with a unique twist - each page begins and ends with a powerful Yantra. Our author firmly believes that there's no better way to organize your days than with these sacred symbols that hold immense significance.

 **Diary:** Introducing the Life Book, your daily planner for the entire year. This diary not only helps you keep track of your schedule but also includes the empowering details of the Power of Yantra. It provides ample space for you to jot down your own quotes, affirmations, and more, making it a truly personalized experience.

 **Sri Yantra Card**: Experience the mind-purifying effects of the Sri Yantra through this special card. Delve into the details of the Yantra and its numerous benefits, ensuring a harmonious and positive journey.

 **Namaste Card:** Unfold the true meaning of the Namaste gesture through this card. Discover that when we bring our hands together, one hand symbolizes our soul, and the other represents Brahman - thus realizing the profound oneness that resides within us.

 **God in Me Card**: This card serves as a profound teacher, reminding us that the divine presence resides within us. Explore the depth of this realization and embrace the divinity that lies at the core of your being.

 **Card on Modiji:** Learn from the life of a man who embodies the wisdom of Ancient philosophy - Sankhya Darshan & Yoga Darshan. Discover the teachings of Sri Narendra Modiji, a small yet impactful way to inspire our youth and adults.

 **Card on Mahavakya:** Unlock the profound wisdom of Mahavakya, which reveals the oneness of the soul and God. Delve into its profound meaning and embrace the unity that connects all beings.

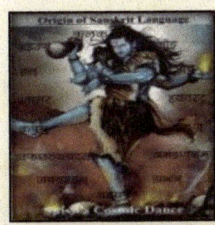
Card on Origin of Sanskrit Language: Unravel the captivating story of the first language in the Universe - Sanskrit. Explore its significance and historical origins, a fascinating tale of linguistic heritage.

Card on Nirvanashatakam: Journey through the powerful verses of Nirvana Shatkam - Aatma Shatkam, a composition by Adi Shankaracharya. Immerse yourself in its teachings, exploring the fundamental question - Who am I? Discover the path to self-realization and inner peace.

Card on Om: Om as a symbol, it represents all aspects of the Universe , manifest and unmanifest. Om is a sound then the whole universe is its vibration. Om is looked upon as a word , it explains all that exists in the universe

Card on Mantra: Mantra is a poetic revelation by human sages during a state of deep concentration. Mantra is like an atomic power. Our Mantra is our real Friend in the world.

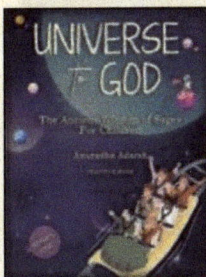
Series 1 – UNIVERSE TO GOD is supported by
Workbook In this children practice wisdom pages of series one Universe to God.

Practice Book In this children practice the teachings of wisdom pages.

                      COMING SOON
         Series 2 :   **Tree of True Self**
         Series 3 :   **Rivers of Thoughts**

Children Are Saying About The Author

Anuradha Aunty

You are kind, sweet and generous. You are very good at teaching. You helped me and you made, made me at the top of the class. You are a good person. You are so nice. And because of you, I have more creativity, knowledge and kindness. Thanks to you, I have so many things to learn and teach. You are funny and taught me the most from all teachers that have taught me. So, from me to you - Thank you from the bottom of my heart. ♥

From - Reva
To - ♥ Aunty

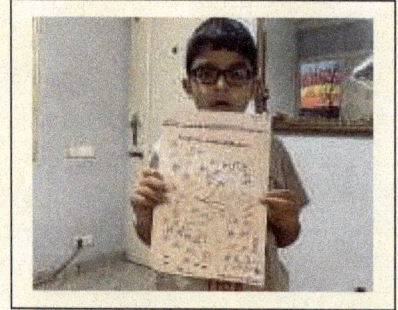
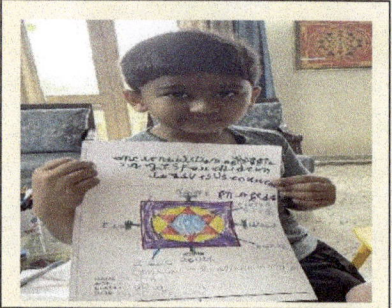

> Thank you Aunty for everything! Ancient wisdom classes and everything else thank you!
>
> ♡ Anandi

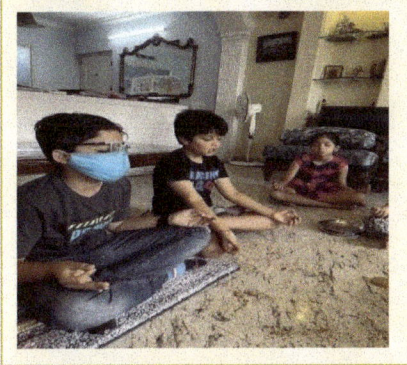

Namaste

My Soul — **Brahman**

One hand is my soul
other hand is Brahman
We are one

www.ingramcontent.com/pod-product-compliance
Lightning Source LLC
LaVergne TN
LVHW070535070526
838199LV00075B/6779